GOOD WANT

GOOD WANT

poetry by

DOMENICA MARTINELLO

COACH HOUSE BOOKS, TORONTO

first edition

 Canada Council Conseil des Arts
for the Arts du Canada

ONTARIO ARTS COUNCIL
CONSEIL DES ARTS DE L'ONTARIO
an Ontario government agency
un organisme du gouvernement de l'Ontario Ontario

Published with the generous assistance of the Canada Council for the Arts
and the Ontario Arts Council. Coach House Books also acknowledges the
support of the Government of Canada through the Canada Book Fund and
the Government of Ontario through the Ontario Book Publishing Tax Credit.

LIBRARY AND ARCHIVES CANADA CATALOGUING IN PUBLICATION

Title: Good want / poetry by Domenica Martinello.
Names: Martinello, Domenica, 1991- author.
Identifiers: Canadiana (print) 2024030070X | Canadiana (ebook)
20240300718 | ISBN 9781552454824 (softcover) | ISBN 9781770568099
(EPUB) | ISBN 9781770568105 (PDF)
Subjects: LCGFT: Poetry.
Classification: LCC PS8626.A77442 G66 2024 | DDC C811/.6—dc23

Good Want is available as an ebook: ISBN 978 1 77056 809 9 (EPUB), 978 1
77056 810 5 (PDF)

To Gino, the best thing I've ever wanted

TABLE OF CONTENTS

I have often thought god needs prayers to remind himself he is important, and still matters. Without our interceding glances, what would he be but a shrunken head on the end of a thread in a museum of ideas?

– *Mary Ruefle*

1.

You do not have to be good.
Being good isn't even the point anymore.
I just don't think it's real
to think of geese and feel so beautiful about yourself
and so far away.

– Hera Lindsay Bird

I PRAY TO BE USEFUL

At the foot of the oratory
I halved my height and
bruised up the stairs.

Each moment is a new
bead to balance on,

and each bead felt
wrongly sumptuous
as I prayed to want less.

Around me people
worked with their hands
and were protected

by the gift of calluses.
Soft and immodest, I created
the world in my image,

inventor of tulips and gold.
I wanted to marry myself

to a profession
of kneeling, to kill
two birds with one stone.

Gardening, cleaning,
tending to babies.
I tried to be useful.

I asked for guidance.
I atoned at each hot step

burning urgently like a secret
UTI. Even on my knees

I could not keep my gaze downcast,
humble, groundward. I could not fast.

Like my hands,
my hunger never
hardened over.

SOLSTICE

Inside my body was a strawberry
stain. Sturdy and sweet, then suddenly
squelched. I choked out everything

that once populated my life.
Summer had no curfew. Flowers died,
public pools dried up and were used

differently. Seeds sprouted all over me,
more magnificent than the mulch of
any teenaged son, teeth looming

in the periphery, canines waiting
to be dyed. I was cruel yet I cried
over everything: my sun-slapped

skin reddening, the roasted pig, gulls
squawking over a hunk of bread,
how slow it took days to grow

dark. I was a daughter plant
squeezing the soft earth too tightly,
trying nightly to will myself green.

I ripened so fast, laid out
on a napkin – now beach towel,
now picnic blanket, now soiled sheet –

the violence of it never ceased
to amaze or deplete.

VAGUE FEAST

or, six sestets one silent

1.

there are many things I want
to do with a paring knife:
unburden the world of its softness,
disrobed in one endless uncoiling peel.
pears are winter fruits, I am
too, whatever you think that means.

2.

it's unwise to leave ripeness unattended.
when I let things go, curses
come back to hurt me. I
left my fruit on a nail
and woke up a spring nettle
begging to be boiled into tea.

3.

minds go loose as fruit flies.
in a summer metaphor juice runs
down the chin of some glib
ancient mountain, ash plastering the hot
and heavy sky, overlooked because she
doesn't know how to dress herself.

4.

I wanted the good want of
girls with their swoony necks, roped
around with friendship. I flashed smooth
lavender beneath my school skirt – nothing.
I hit myself against their numb
popsicle lips and erupted into hives.

5.

... ...
... ...
... ...
... ...
... ...
... ...

6.

the leaves lisp girlishly to me.
in windy solidarity I am open
to any and all secrets. trees
rehearsing the voice of seeds on
a thread, I fashion my own
necklace. sow it to my neck.

GOOD EYE

The eye is the lamp of your body; when your eye is clear, your whole body also is full of light; but when it is bad, your body also is full of darkness. – Luke 11:34

I turn my special eye to god's many opportunities,

which only we are blessed to see. Rotting pumpkin,

dead pigeon, god's palm,

pink and wrinkly as a bite mark

in days-old gum, god's backhand.

The temperature drops so low oil turns to ice in the pantry.

Our windows are saran-wrapped. Air this cold is a portal,

the snap of an elastic band. My dad and I play a distraction game

to stay thankful to live in a place where seasons change.

We see who can spot more burnt-out Christmas lights.

We walk on shouting the score,

feet sore, until god's wind cuts out our tongues

like an aftertaste, Granny Smith laced with glass.

Then we appreciate the silence.

When the sky dims and violets by 4 p.m. you need to stare hard

at the bone-faced sun while you can. Then add it to the tally.

Our street is lined with a million cracked balconies

I see myself falling through.

BUTTER RECEPTACLE

I like the admin work, I like zip-locking, the ad libbing, the serenades at nap time, killing a game of charades, feeding two birds with one scone, letting the cats keep their skin, finding a way, breaking capsules on my face, disappearing veins, the oil pull, the masking, the flushing, the versatility of mould, its flirty fuzz, black or white, wet or fluffy, spores, s'mores by the radiator, I like the blackened popcorn, the microwaved tang, the robust ghost of a thousand smells, I like the clink-clanking, I like spinning and dancing, I like the gratitude journaling, the prancing around, tittering, online bra shopping, tube-topping, gin-soaking, milk bath, floating daisies, upset flora, old floors, the unbalanced PH, inflation-rate character build, the salty swelling, the landlord's rich croissants, ancestral sourdough starter, all-purpose bleach, I like the vinegar cocktail recipe, another thing checked off the laundry list, you get the gist, I like note taking, I like to categorize, synthesize, synergize, mudslide, wrestle, sling my digital grocery order, sing into my budgeting app-slash-ovulation tracker, I like my eggs by the door, I like the happy blueberry-fed chickens, eating more fresh fruit than me, preening and plucky, paying their way, so much younger and less afraid.

POWER BALLAD (HYMN)

My body is
a metaphor
of the body

as a landscape
cluttered with loaves
and fish in baskets.

I'll never be
conceptual.
I am one

with the masses.
Like, imagine following through?
I mean *all the way* through…

One day you'll wake up in a room
where no one else grew up poor

and they'll call this a success.
You can write

grant applications about it.
Tell the nice officer of the arts
about the time your dad

took the metro at midnight
to Burger King
on Christmas Eve

but make it a metaphor
about piety and meat.
I assume all artists are lying

and I lie too.
I swear my life feels
meaningful sometimes.

I've stretched baloney, conceptually,
as far as it can be stretched.
I commit myself

to showing my work
even if the answer is wrong

in the end.
I live inside

big intentions.
All this is

my bread
and butter.

HOT PUMP

Thoreau said *know your own*
bone. I dissolve mine in vinegar

Still, I try to speak pretty.

Pretend to be civilized
while gnawing on what's left
of my own right arm.

Be both handmaid and host.

Serve cocktail weenies
in the stylized carapace
of a grand palatial home.

Watch me pickle
in pilfered liquor

like both sets of ancestors.

Appearing presentable to guests
as they glide through my life,

I tenderize the tough
muscle of my tongue.

Channel all the spirits,

sugar, water, bitters.
Think of my great-grandmother,
a bootlegging Quebecer

who rubbed way more than shoulders
with the cosmopolitan rich.

Whose English sounded like
crushing peanuts under a bar stool.

Who wrapped God around her like a mink coat
in the rude reprieve of old age.

Then the lazzarone churn
of my lazy Neapolitan blood,
like steak drippings licked
off a stranger's plate.

Gorgeous and drunk,
the alley their bedroom,
the ocean their bidet.

Salt-of-the-earth countrymen,
paid to pave, steal, and snitch.

In callused tanned hands,
the whole world on a dish.

Eating rats and caviar,
eels and snakes, beating
their wives, teeth stained

with dregs of homemade wine.
We all turned out just fine.

The hot pump of industry
and a slow, murky lethargy
wind equally through my body.

Visitors patronize
the rooms of my life

and I could suck the marrow
out of each one with a straw.

Me, a pretend intellectual,
ruthless and ineffectual.

An airhead without airs,
drinking piss from silverware,

I lock spectators
in the unfinished basement
for a good, long think.

Here's a kernel to grind:
Money can't buy class.
It's inherited genetically.

Tough titties,
my ancestors might say.

Boo-hoo for you.

I inherited secrecy
like a rash.

Turn the bone to rubber.

No one leaves here
till it's scratched.

• • •   • • •   • • •   • • •   • • •   • • •

IN BAD DREAMS

I clock in

for my evil night shift

Sewers flood with blood

(This is definitely my fault)

Tigers roam the alley

ripping toddlers apart

like a dog with a well-loved plushie

(I am solely responsible)

Among the recurring

pathological crimes

I forget to feed pets

usually a series of birds, cats, or bunnies

and by the time I realize this fact

my tortured little vessels of psyche

have starved for weeks but cannot die

What does it mean

to dream in the cadence of animal

suffering, in the refrain

of oops, how did that happen

again

Then again

why does everything need to say something

The hot doctoral candidate in my head

says, *Why not*

in that perfect existential tone

He trilingual, cunnilingual, knows how to cook

in that accomplished, undomestic way

Yeah I guess so, I say

I'm just so tired of trying to be meaningful

I just want to say nothing

but throw some weight behind it

Y'know?

(He did not know)

Well

Have you ever contemplated

the administrative burden

of being alive?

Yes

but my wide-hipped wife came with a dowry

a lavender field

empire, actually

with many subordinates

and supporters, assistants and adjuncts,

helpers, advisors, coordinators, financial backers,

hair combers and project managers, wet nurses,

scullery maids –

Now I put a pillow over his face

I love pillow time

I wish I could go

all the way

My bad dreams are lit and boxed

in like hours on the retail sales floor

suspended indefinitely in the refrain

of boring, ongoing pain

I prick the meat

of my breast with a name tag

(The PhD candidate smirks at this)

ouch

I punch the clock

bloody

Misting my wrists with sleep

spray and praying

that all these little gods

finally die

2.

I have no ambitions or desires.
Being a poet is not my ambition.
It's my way of being alone.

– *Alberto Caeiro (Fernando Pessoa),*
trans. Margaret Jull Costa and Patricio Ferrari

I PRAY TO THE PALE FIRE

There's a life
inside my life

that's pale
as fuck

from having never
seen the sun.

At night I feel
its contours

as I sleep,
pressing up

against the inside
of my cheek.

I hide this life
intensely.

Think up analogies
for it in my dreams –

Russian doll,
ongoing pregnancy,

a snake struggling
to shed its coil.

This version is
most hopeful.

If I continue
bashing my face

against the rock,
learn to slither out

of this shameful
nylon sock

of skin, one day
the life inside

my life might
finally be free

to wake up as it is:
scaled and dewy.

To swallow any
other life at will.

To sprawl like a sheath
of muscle, sunbathing

on a rock.
Asleep I flick and lash

the air from memory
and face the forked

path like an old enemy
before eating my own tail.

PLAYING HOUSE

We don't bog ourselves down
in the details of make-believe.
Sometimes I'm mommy, sometimes I'm daddy.

We are each only a girl
pressing hands flatly together.
I slink beneath her body
like a cat under a car.

Dew in her peachy moustache,
legs stiff as a steeple, I smell
the wood-varnished crucifix
above the frilly single bed

and her breath flushing my cheek.
Transubstantiated and scorched
behind the eyes, I'm
suddenly alive and wilful

with questions, like why
she asked me to walk on her
back once, the way her father
walked on her mother's

in the middle of the night.
She'd wriggled under my bare feet.
My greasy handprints balancing
against the white wall of their den

and what did it mean?
The mnemonic for the sign of the cross
was the first poem we ever learned
from the old nuns in Sunday school:

spectacles, testicles, wallet, watch.
Mysterious, silly, full of adult significance.

We lay together like that,
lightly, still in our uniforms.
A quartet of simple parts,
motions for the big undefined.

From memory, she touches
her forehead to mine,
stomach, left shoulder,
right shoulder.

ASKING FOR IT

I got every good thing in
life by asking for it, and

every bad thing too – or so
they'd have me believe.

Poetry often feels to me like
clicking the beads of a rosary.

It's not hurting anybody, I guess,
but that doesn't make it virtuous.

I've no faith in the abacus
or alphabet, a meek and useless

sonnet. Still, I sit counting
syllables like cards, hoping to pull

a fast one. Doing nothing while wanting
the whole world to do more.

ALL THE TRIMMINGS

I like something from nothing. I like looking
at all the pretty bottles before food comes at the restaurant.
We even eat the garnish. Peel the plastic fruit in the plastic bowl.
Chip our teeth on ceramic lemons.

I like this lesson. *Waste not, want not.* Waste not your wanting.
We want more of everything. Clutch our coupons and say nothing.
Skip silently down long aisles of winter.
Freeze our fingers picking bottles for coins.

I like something from nothing when nothing tastes so fruity
with bubbles. I like the clinking in the fridge. Everywhere weather
exists, we exist to endure it.
Aspire to trim. I like being sturdy for no reason.

Looking at the pretty bottles, we fold our hands in happy grace.
What a thrill to be a garnish. A sprig of noble nothing.

A bag of kitchen scraps. Shovels scratch the frozen earth.
We bury offerings in sacks. Subsist on melon rinds
and onion skins and rusty cans.
Stiffen modestly to say, *It's nothing.*

LITTLE LIGHT

I want a pool that is the world.

I want to jump on a trampoline in my backyard.

The movies told me there'd be
pools and trampolines,

pancakes in the morning before school.
There'd be bathtubs and staircases,

a dignified breed of family dog
to guard my door at night.

I swear somewhere down the line
someone promised there'd be scuba diving.

I thought there'd be a film,
some protective coating.

Yet I stand in my life,
a raw sunburned nerve.

I chase a patch of shade
as the chain-link slaps
patterns across my face

like a yearning knock-off
purse. I want cedar bushes,
a saltwater pool.

I want a loft
bed with a desk underneath,
a telescope trained at the moon

ordered from a catalogue,
a hammock to disappear into.
A pretty view, a little garden.

I'll settle for some landscaping.
Okay, I'll settle for the landscape.
Every day I settle

for the public
playground
where I escape
and manifest.

Climb into a scratched neon tube,
the air hot and plastic.
Live in the park's plumbing,
a small comma in the pipes.

Knees to face, feet on the graffiti,
tunnels of *fucks* and slurs and phone numbers,
call Stacey for a good time.

Reverberating chatter,
the echo in a home
with long hallways.

Sealed up and away
from concrete and sand.

Alone and overcrowded.

A little light comes through a burn hole.

I put my eye to its eye.

SILENT RETREAT

I stopped to listen. The housedresses listened back.
My ear cradled to her low-heeled leather shoe, panicked

tones from outside the door. Time was slow
and specific. I spoke into an imaginary receiver

that was once a calf grazing on the plains.
I wanted to hide for a few more minutes

before accepting my fate
for ripping the plastic covers off all the new

expensive chairs. In the closet something changed
my station: the hot fact of her breath, her eye

observing through a crack in the wood.
I never noticed it was blue. She left me

alone, undisturbed, in collusion with her things,
now one of them. Between then and today

there's a bridge. When your elders die
you're one step closer.

Her dresses hanging limp, simple,
anonymous. Parcelled off, undescribed.

Unrecognizable furniture kicked
to matchsticks on the curb.

The dial tone, a vast vagueness,
soft skin leathering, voiceless, nameless,

gentle like a hymn, softly
rubbing out each footprint.

WE KEEP SUNLIGHT IN THE BASEMENT

We're shown how
to stow extra for a rainy day
It involves couponing.

If anything, we slip sunlight
into our purses, down our slips,

line shelves with it like gold
in the tackiest shades of yellow.
We all know there are limits

to sunlight and who gets to feel it.
We bathe in it, pure and citric.

We accumulate, cultivate,
multiply. There's never enough
and nothing it can't do. Mothers

make you gargle it to speak clean
and pretty. It dapples our floors,

our babies, our hard callused feet.
My kin consult their almanacs. Predict
floods, famines, and disasters,

nursing their unseasonable
wartime mentalities we forgive them for,

their stubborn wills to live.
Squeaking by, degreasing, delousing,
ritual washings each Sunday.

In the history of sunlight, it is said
two brothers brought this liquid candour

into our homes. My family is full
of dramatic stories involving two brothers.
Somehow our glasses are sparkling.

The world pricks our eyes
and whispers, *keep stockpiling.*

Sunlight is a sign of life for people
who live in basements and cracks,
imagine juice out of powder, tide out

of detergent, wine out of water.
Amassing is a creative act.

The dream of a future in which we
refuse to show up empty-handed.
Bright and primal, this fear

for tomorrow, faith in a world
in which someone will need

the small comfort of washing a dish.

CIRCLING BACK

I lock fingers with myself, preteen. I offer up the underwire. I bounce and supple, drag and drop the pretense, steal. My fanny pack is plump, I smell all pungent and powdery. I return to puppy shampoo, milk and strawberries. I roll in the knoll and sniff my grassy knees. I scorch and sample, run and snot, suck face at the bus stop with a Halls in my cheek. I bleed. I bray and heel, pee in strong spurts that never burn. I fur and yearn, stretch and rip. All shirts are belly shirts. Punctured and pierced, I stud, shred, and patch. I serrate and wheedle, huff puny highs and experiment with cuts. I ache. I crawl home with hair under my tongue. Sip cough syrup in the quiet of a bush. I have a mission. I produce coins to procure fries. Get the shakes. Steam and flush and pillow fight. I sugar and grease with prurient delight, stink and cream, frolic all sticky in the feathers. I tip the nozzle to my mouth, swirl, spritz, gorge, spit. I poke holes. I punch. Thumb my thumbs through the sleeves I've wrecked. Stomp my eyes with the heels of my palms. I do uncouth things with hot glue. Murals left undone, recklessly staple-gunned, coffee souring under the bed. The uneaten lunch stuffed in the doorless closet, mossy with fluff. Years without the privilege of privacy, unhinged, opened, punished. We're soft, we're angry, we're spoiled, we've written mean things in our diaries. I know it all and I know nothing. I reach through the beaded doorway. I tell myself a secret.

••• ••• ••• ••• ••• •••

SLEEP IS TRYING TO TELL ME SOMETHING

something about

all the badness of which I am capable?

Oh yeah

Sure, it starts innocent enough

When things slip your mind

like a silk scrunchie

up the crook

of your arm and the evil deeds

seep in, all gosh golly

and polite

a cowboy holding

the elevator gate with a gun

in his underwear

like some retelling

of Kafka's 'Before the Law'

Here's what you need to know

I will strike

little deals with myself not to lie

for no reason

and call that 'having

integrity'

It's all very civilized

There are other clauses and stipulations

lusty little loopholes

that you shouldn't look at too directly

Despite my great yawping psyche

I've kept and fed animals

Things have kept and fed me

When I feed squirrels at the park

I admit I'm still afraid

the nice ones have rabies

My mom told me that as a kid

keep your distance

it's the calm ones

the cunning ones

the ones quick to approach you

alone on a bench

the ones that walk around like *I own this park,*

princess

Give me your ice cream cone

and I give it

exposing my fingers

to rabies with no hesitation

In the park as a kid

my nonna picked up a pigeon

with her bare hands

We named it Charlie

Our neighbour saw

called her filthy

yelled obscenities

called her a smelly wop

I'll never forget that word

smelly

She was not above putting a live animal in her purse

throwing the cat off the balcony

slipping a bloody steak down the front of her dress

But she was so good

no you don't understand

It's just this whole thing

Some years there are horse metaphors

even for those of us

with zero access to a horse

mortadella pearling our days

with fatty spots sliced translucent and thin

Other years snakeskin makes a comeback

In the era before I was born

my other grandma worked a hotel bar

with a gentlemen's club in the basement

She loved issuing cheques to the strippers

Only good girls get cheques

Maybe this is obvious

but drawing a straight line

takes a confidence I can't afford

I'm done with it

I just want the parts

The icing, the filling

Thick slabs of baloney

between buttered bread

The elementary school teacher in my heads says,

Honey

How is everything at home

Her name is Nancy

Why can't Nancy and everyone

just leave me the hell alone

3.

I am no good
Goodness is not the point anymore
Holding on to things
Now that's the point

— *Dorothea Lasky*

I PRAY IN SCREAMERS HOUSE OF HORRORS

Part of me
was still on the party bus

with the estranged branch of my family.

Part of me swallowed a wavy
strand of the Niagara Falls.

It rappelled down my throat
like coloured scarves, each knot

a repentance, resentment lost,

while part of me clicked a padlock closed
on the redemption arc for luck.

Part of me was gleeful
at unsnapping the twig and reversing the tape.

Part of me knew the blood was fake
as the dark tunnel shrieked in August heat.

On my knees in the hooded canal, whites turn blue
and bare their teeth at the part of me begging

myself to heal without giving the trick away.

Under the strobe lights, plucking my nerves
like a crunched popsicle, part of me was promised

a celebratory pin, *I made it through*

Screamers House of Horrors,
even after all of this.

Part of me rolled my eyes

through the roadblock of ghosts
and skeletons lined up

for a strike. Part of me hit the gutter
hard and came out the other side

into whoops and hollers, pats on the back,
smacked with the black, beaming flashlight

of forgiveness.

While part of me did not believe, not for
one fucking second, in all of that

terrible business.

CON

My first time

in a confessional

I was so small I

fit under the sink.

The lord's house had no

air conditioning.

We had this in common.

I went through my Sunday training

resentful, sweating and pale

as a lump of mozzarella.

Provoked and prodded for weeks

before the booth, I balled

my fists, wracked my brain, finally

apologized for saying a bad word.

Repeated it gleefully

as the holy father told me,

That's not how

confessions work.

My stomach growled

a low, evil frequency

only the kids licking their fingers

in the nearby pews could hear.

BAD EYE

The eye is the lamp of your body; when your eye is clear, your whole body also is full of light; but when it is bad, your body also is full of darkness. – Luke 11:34

Snapshot: gold ring in the mud underneath the old deck.

The house sold, their tall blond children fled. I once coveted

a ring from one of them, muscular and goofy, all smile, no bite.

He swallowed my contact lenses in a glass on the nightstand,

fell in love as I pegged him on his childhood bed.

I accidentally snuck into a perfect summer.

Called his dad 'Dad.'

Was rich with euphemisms for the nuclear family.

Dinners outside; fanning a blown-out polaroid; jizzy

scentless soap; pumping a salad spinner; the backyard jacuzzi.

Rolled between the slats, I fidgeted away the heirloom

I inherited from someone's second divorce. Spinning it like a dial

that finally popped open. Things ended abruptly inside its eye.

All things.

Probably its sinister radiation is what ended that nice family

and likely the next, given the statistics.

I leave the humid memory and turn off the flash. I exit into the icy

held breath of the present. For one perfect second

it tastes like a frozen grape.

The sky is so black it's like god capped her camera

and couldn't bear to watch. It takes only one blurred image

to shake me – god is running, being chased.

Her camera bag's bouncing all over the place.

PARABLE

I crawled across
the bottom of the lake
after my blind date.

Grew bold as I accumulated

seaweed, detritus.
Sand caking my face like a mask
I'd never stop staring at.

I was a tourist in this city, my body.

Caught a reflection in the glass facade of a bank.

Became the bank, the glass, the light.

TONGUE AND GROOVE

Dimensional biographer,
my desk is a door.
It's a bathroom door.
I've got five dollars
and each dollar smells
like a syllable
oozing here in the great white North.
My imagined breakfasts
are an expensive dedication to you,
chronicler, contractor, new clique.
I live to be easy.
I made this ink
inside my body,
both of which are invisible.
Serve a pancake over the gash
in my forehead
leading directly into a volcano
peppered with summer tongs
and other hot accessories.
My brain jiggles suggestively
for you, my machete.
If I want to be elevated
I'll twirl
the pepper grinder.
I rent my eggnog French toast
and forget my own needs,
make wood into shapes,
add a special ingredient
that changes nothing whatsoever.
Forget to be lettered.

Once stained and finished and rendered,
it's easy to forget
the broken eggs.
I'm the paper under your leg
keeping the whole thing steady.
Fell a tree.
Use my pinky.
Have you been counting?
Stressed, unstressed.
There's still something
to undress in this
scrambled carpentry.

INFINITY MIRROR

my grandma gongs the gong and is cancer-free
but says she still gets all the perks

a plastic jewel unsews itself from her knock-off
ed hardy cap as the crowd claps and hands her a coffee

someone at the condo comes up once a night to wash her back
she throws a bag of cheese curds at the walmart cashier

is honoured in facebook posts
by a few of her kids that still speak to her

alive and owning computers
defying all the odds of their childhoods

through the power of pure delusion
she chain-smokes romance novels

I opened one to a random page
found a single grey pubic hair

I was inside her
inside my mom

who was inside with my aunt
who had my cousins inside of her

such is the swell of biology
all the eggs and follicles

this random magical business
dressed down and destroyed

unsewn from reality
not a gong

or a conjuring
it's a myth in kitsch

no not kitsch
trash

cheap trash
when you're hungry

it's a feast.

I TURN THIRTY FAR FROM THE COAST

My mother clamped down her grief
and was delivered to the doctors.

She'd trained herself to prevent sudden loss.
The durational rigour of a six-month bedrest,

steadying her breath, evening her pulse.
Only for loss to come wet and gruesome

as she imagined, but impossibly removed.
Because she was so sick, I have no photos

of her pregnant, but there are other proofs.
Like how tightly her mind held me

as I stretched it. How lightning scored
her body recording my shape.

When I think of generosity,
I see its slow pace.

Blankets in a dim room
rising quietly, dough under a cloth.

Her father drowned on a business trip
and I lived to imagine it, the green fit of rage.

A sea nymph sucking him down
like an oyster on my birthday.

With age I've come to know nothing
mythological ever happens in Florida.

We're tied to our common fates.
To endure, landlocked, where

he was put into the earth,
that abstract watering place.

IT FOLLOWS

What good is a backwards glance?
Lot's wife looked and became the
pillar of her community. Orpheus looked.

Now his head sings on a spike.
I refuse to be useful only
in the rear-view of my strife.

ON THE DAY MARY OLIVER DIED

in January I flee
back to the mid-moan
of summer

leaving Gino talking
to himself in the kitchen
with frosted windows

cracking like two cubes
in a glass of hard water

have you ever had a girlhood
with palms so sweaty
the bus pole dripped?

~

BEWT: Bodies Experiencing Weather Together

wow
believe me
I find sunsets interesting

if you don't find it
profound please pretend

what if the soft
animal of my body
is a little Shih Tzu
I've never loved?

on the bus
free-bleeding near the boys and my comrade
the dripping bus pole

yes this is where I decide to go
to period town
sweater tied around my waist

next to my best friend who I miss
just far enough away

    that the sun and clear pebbles of rain
    move differently

bumpy landscape of our lives
all our years up to no good

                and the final transformation:

                    two big dogs
                    and a husband
                    in the country

                    an actual family
                    and a mortgage
                    that sweet spot

where sunsets over the lake are never cliché

where the local weed dealer plays with your kids at the BBQ

it's as good as it gets

and I never said I was good

~

meanwhile the world goes on

hands plunged into the soapy sink water of it all

my body's a little pageant dog

yes I am Lacey
with a bow in my hair
eating my own shit

barking at my shadow
and losing a fight
with some geese at the park

I lose all my friends to mortgages and big dogs in the country

meanwhile I need to be carried
everywhere in a purse

playing dead
to be adored

I can do backflips too
I am versatile like that
always asking the big questions like

am I just some art school bitch
who finds sunsets 'commonplace'
or am I dissociating under beauty
like a lush velvet cape

~

once my high school boyfriend told me
the more beautiful a sunset the more likely
we'd all die of smog poisoning

I thought he was *sooooo* smart
and then he paid for our pad thai

in university I gave a presentation on Mary Oliver
and the prof poked fun at me

if our poetic influences are our chosen family

you're gonna go with … Mary Oliver

okaaaaay …

I thought they were so smart
a true intellectual
a true intellectual for dunking on someone like me

~

meanwhile Gino pets my smelly fur

he's both carrying the bag
and in the bag with me
so even if I'm humiliated
I never feel lonely

meanwhile I live in the city
we have weather here too

I announce my place   in the prairies and deep trees
                                     clotting the gutter of my imagination
                                     that imperfect escape hatch

if you find this trite that's on you
blood drips pastorally down my leg

~

                                           whoever you are

you're there with me too

••• ••• ••• ••• ••• •••

THE HORSES EAT APPLES

Snakes eat apples

I eat apple crisp

after a wholesome trip to the farm

We all tend our little orchards

awash in the knowledge

of all this badness

(I put Cool Whip on it)

Somewhere inside the hideous

wallpapered chamber of my heart

working so hard to pump out

good blood

my grandma sits cheering

on an exotic dancer from rural Ontario

paying her way through vet school

and leaves my mom hiding in a closet

for three days without food

I want to bake my mom

into an apple pie

to keep her safe

Something sweet and macabre

an iconic image

is a thing forced to go on meaning forever

self-feeding and refusing to die

Some people can go their whole life being 'good'

having never had the impulse

to swallow an apple whole

Lodging it in the larynx

for future contemplation

I make everyone uncomfortable

waiting for someone to reach in with their teeth

and free it

Who will bob for my apples

Few have tried

I put a pillow over their face

Few have ignored the bulging mass

All the better

Through the glory of evolution

it is now a mere physiological fact of me

fermented through the world's vileness

this throatful of sweet vinegar

bit my dad like a feral cat

Rifled through a friend's trash

considered pocketing a used maxi-pad

Played Chat Roulette do you remember that

Never invited friends over

with their stupid fucking pools

Chugged vanilla extract

Smoked the deep oregano of my shame

Faked literally everything you can imagine

Felt jealous of friends who practised kissing on each other

Masturbated on the phone with an unsuspecting caller

Saw a poster of Jack Layton and imagined my mom

in the oven

Am I winning the vulnerability Olympics

by admitting that if everyone who loves me

would just let go and die

I might be free

to not seek some higher purpose

or lower to a sense of duty

Tell myself

Good for you, you deserve a good time

You can't afford not to!

Lick the plate

Eat the whole bag

It's called investing in yourself

I must take this risk

Indulge my selfishness

Allow myself this badness

Protect the hoard of fruit flies

swimming up from the drainpipe

I can't explain it, just trust me

It is better to live without shame

and I instantly regret it

but it doesn't need to make sense

Unburdened by literal thinking

only some of these are lives

Only some of these are lies

I only lie sometimes

And I always have my reasons.

4.

I wanted
the past to go away, like another country; I wanted
my life to close, and open like a hinge …
I wanted
to hurry into the work of my life; I wanted to know,
whoever I was, I was

alive
for a little while.

– Mary Oliver

GOOD WANT

Good is what happens
when you stretch God too far.

And who am I
to eat margarine

in the dark cupboard
of my aliveness?

~

What I want is generic.

A good, cheap stretch.
Nylon, spandex, whatever
the hell jeggings are made from.

From a certain distance
it all looks the same.

Specificity worn abstract,
just outside my range

and squinted at prettily

like some random flowers
in the supple folds of a field.

Like a camel toe on display
in a pair of name-brand jeans.

There are right and wrong
ways to catalogue the past.

Parasuco, Bongo,
Levi's, Guess.

Living things repeat.
I continue to guess

at God's limberness,
his jealous eye
for tight beauty.

What I want
is more

forgiving.

~

Want is what happens.

The verb enters your heel
like a brown shard of glass.

Next comes shame.

~

Rearrange my household's
fast fashions: *good, bad,*
these, those,

whatever, whomever.
Utility feels safe.

Rounded, functional,
all-encompassing –
there's comfort

in letting things go
if they're easily replaced.

I don't want new words
for old feelings.
I have no commitment

to polishing or passing down
an idiosyncratic upkeep.

~

I roll italics around the back of my throat.

What, yes, no, beauty.
A knack for making *something* from *umm*

and *nothing* from *oh,*
all easy to swallow.

Then came the fear,
horribly specific. Of what

would slide out of me
if I dared unclench

and live.

—

Vagueness was a friend
of God.

Then came the big, baggy dread.

We all know where the details
get you.

'Castigate,' a word
like a chestnut

roasting in the scalding
pits of hell.

My mother had a *bad* childhood.
I've trained myself to kill it

with beautifully curated
charcuterie boards.

～

God squeezed
my father's feet

into vague shapes
by withholding.

We grow around
our constraints.

I dream of smoothing
out his callused toes

like uncrumpling
a losing lottery ticket.

～

What does it mean,
to want good things?

～

To envy your newborn,
wishing you could suck your own tit?

To eat figs from a tree down the road?
To pray to saints for baby boys?

To move to Canada by boat?
To spike the milk with rice

when there's nothing left?
To push up the concrete

like the roots of a petulant tree
when the daily sky tries

to pave over you? To hit your spade
against the frozen earth?

To dig up garbage in your own backyard
each spring? To watch your children grow

old and stop maintaining everything
you've worked so hard to give?

~

In my fantasies,
I intervene.

I'm alive in the seventies
to fulfill my destiny

as the helpful neighbour
in this scene:

lovely twin girls
neglected and budding,

braless and feral,
scared of all the wrong things.

My future little mother,
my future little auntie.

Will you come in for a pop
and some chips?

I have a full fridge
and my door has a lock.

Do I need to get into specifics
for you to witness what this is?

~

To order what you're craving without looking at the price?

To dream of big windows and never paying rent?

To steal a squash from the grocery store?

To smarten up and steal a roast chicken next?

To add water to expired cake mix and pretend it's your birthday?

To hope someone sees you?

To wonder why no one intervenes?

To believe all the ugly words?

To grow around the silence in a misshapen mass?

To marry someone just as misshapen because who else would understand?

To have a baby and give her your world?

To give her your world with all the ugly parts italicized?

To put needles in your face?

To bathe yourself in olive oil?

To be on the work wellness committee?

To order gold jewellery online for no reason?

To survive it?

To then live alone and age?

—

God said, Let there be light.
And all that's good said, No.

—

Growing up, we always lived
in apartments across from parks

to make the public space our own.
Held by its noisy joy,

I stretched my limbs
toward the lilac bushes

where junkies dropped
their syringes.

I live inside my small life
alongside the city seagulls

and write myself out
into the peaceful, open field.

—

A table for eating, a clock for measuring time,
the sturdy boon of the status quo.

I'm turning down the volume.
I'm loosening the metaphor

that ties things together, give it
away like the ribbon of a balloon.

Like the ribbons of balloons
I used to kiss and send to heaven

after our special trips to Pizza Hut.

~

The specifics don't matter.

I appreciate the flat surface to eat on, whether floor or chest.

I appreciate the yeast of time rising like a steam off the earth.

I forgive you for not understanding this loose gesture,

as I forgive *everyone, everything.*

As I hope you'll forgive me

if you understand it all too much.

~

God, bless this strange bread. I accept
the dough I've been given.

I am the caretaker of *good* and *bad*
and I loosen their reins.

⁓

Living things repeat,
I am alive.

⁓

Continue kneading the world
with my small, specific life.

••• ••• ••• ••• ••• •••

CASINO WORLD

Be strong Domenica
Nobody will ever know
the bets we've made to be here

against our better judgment
and tendency to play the penny slots

to hold back and say *no thanks*
to plink down little tokens
and go home lighter

without really having lost anything
to Big Bertha, Da Vinci Diamonds,
Divine Fortune, Casino World

There is great shame in having a secret
pinkie finger circling the word *more*

when all you thought you wanted
was to drink free coffee and stare

at the flashing lights, Necromancer,
Lucky Ladies, Wild Wheel Big Money,
Valley of the Gods, Vikings

Go to Hell, and it's about time
to unclench your lever-pulling fist
to stop creating a myth out of everything

and admit it, you're greedy
and in love

with a nose so straight and trustworthy
it should be minted
on a golden coin

Admit to wanting to hide
him under your tongue or else
in the socket of your eye

where he shines wildly

because you'd die if you slipped
him into a narrow slot

and denied the ridiculous
stakes you both deserve

we've ascended to the upper floors
we chip

at our fear
bubbled and cracked

under layers of bad paint jobs,
Blaze of Ra, Pirate's Charm, Golden
Colts, Book of the Dead, you're approaching

that high-rolling feeling now
and keep approaching it

faithfully, Double Diamond,
Dancing Drums, Cleopatra, all the stars
in the sky like bingo dabbers

Domenica, when you learned
to say *no*

that was your power

And when you learned to say *yes*
and to keep on saying it

That was your power too

NOTES

p. 9: From 'My Private Property' in *My Private Property* by Mary Ruefle.

p. 11: From 'Wild Geese by Mary Oliver by Hera Lindsay Bird' in *Hera Lindsay Bird* by Hera Lindsay Bird.

p. 37: From '1' in *The Complete Works of Alberto Caeiro*, edited by Jerónimo Pizarro and Patricio Ferrari, translated by Margaret Jull Costa and Patricio Ferrari.

p. 61: From 'Ars Poetica' in *Black Life* by Dorothea Lasky.

pp. 77–81: 'On the Day Mary Oliver Died' borrows lines or near lines from Mary Oliver's 'Wild Geese.'

p. 89: From 'Dogfish' in *Dream Work* by Mary Oliver.

pp. 103–105: 'Casino World' riffs on Bernadette Mayer's 'The Way to Keep Going in Antarctica' and adopts a version of the opening lines. The proper nouns in the poem are popular slot machines.

GOOD THANKS

To the editors of the following publications who gave earlier versions of these poems a small, specific life of their own: *Arc Poetry Magazine*, *The Bennington Review*, *Black Warrior Review*, *carte blanche*, *The Columbia Review*, *The Commuter*, *Contemporary Verse 2*, *Maisonneuve*, *The Malahat Review*, *Poetry Northwest*, PRISM *International*, ROOM *Magazine*, *Salt Hill Journal*, *The South Carolina Review*, *The Walrus*, and *Weird Era*.

To the judges of the *Malahat Review*'s Long Poem Prize, Bertrand Bickersteth and Jennifer Lynn Still, for selecting 'Good Want' as a winner in 2023. I'd also like to thank Iain Higgins, Jolene Loveday, and the rest of the readers and team.

To early readers, editors, and others who shaped this book: Gwen Aube, Adéle Barclay, D. M. Bradford, Jake Byrne, S. Brook Corfman, Bronwyn Haney, Susan Holbrook, Marcela Huerta, Sruti Islam, T. Liem, James Lindsay, Alex Manley, Cassidy McFadzean, Tara McGowan-Ross, Adrian Ngai, Ben Rowley, Crystal Sikma, Candace De Taeye, Lauren Turner, Shy Watson, Alana Wilcox, Lindsay Yates, and many more.

To the Canada Council for the Arts and the Conseil des arts et des lettres du Québec for their generous support. It's made protecting a part of my life for writing a continued possibility.

To the people populating said life and making it meaningful: my husband, my parents, my in-laws, my aunts and uncles, my chosen siblings, my nieces and nephews, my godson.

You make me believe in something greater.

Domenica Martinello is a writer from Montreal, Quebec, and the author of *All Day I Dream About Sirens* (2019). She holds an MFA from the Iowa Writers' Workshop, where she was the recipient of the Deena Davidson Friedman Prize for Poetry.

Domenica was a finalist for the 2017 RBC Bronwen Wallace Award for Emerging Writers and served as a judge for the award in 2021. In 2023, she won the *Malahat Review*'s Long Poem Prize for her sequence 'Good Want.'

For her prose writing, Domenica won the carte blanche 3Macs Prize for a genre-bending work of literary criticism on Elena Ferrante, and has published reviews and criticism in the *Globe and Mail*, *Montreal Review of Books*, *Canadian Notes & Queries*, and elsewhere.

Typeset in Arno and Gotham.

Printed at the Coach House on bpNichol Lane in Toronto, Ontario, on Zephyr Antique Laid paper, which was manufactured, acid-free, in Saint-Jérôme, Quebec, from second-growth forests. This book was printed with vegetable-based ink on a 1973 Heidelberg KORD offset litho press. Its pages were folded on a Baumfolder, gathered by hand, bound on a Sulby Auto-Minabinda, and trimmed on a Polar single-knife cutter.

Coach House is located in Toronto, which is on the traditional territory of many nations, including the Mississaugas of the Credit, the Anishnabeg, the Chippewa, the Haudenosaunee, and the Wendat peoples, and is now home to many diverse First Nations, Inuit, and Métis peoples. We acknowledge that Toronto is covered by Treaty 13 with the Mississaugas of the Credit. We are grateful to live and work on this land.

Edited by t. liem
Cover and interior design by Crystal Sikma
Author photo by Vincenzo D'Alto

Coach House Books
80 bpNichol Lane
Toronto ON M5S 3J4
Canada

mail@chbooks.com
www.chbooks.com